ETHEL BARRETT

tells Favorite Bible Stories

Regal Books

A Division of GL Publications
Ventura, CA U.S.A.

The foreign language publishing of all Regal books is under the direction of Gospel Literature International (GLINT). GLINT provides financial and technical help for the adaptation, translation and publishing of books for millions of people worldwide. For information regarding translation, contact: GLINT, P.O. Box 6688, Ventura, California 93006.

Third Printing, 1982

Published by Regal Books
A Division of GL Publications
Ventura, California 93006
Printed in U.S.A.

Library of Congress Catalog Card No. 77-93051
ISBN 0-8307-0615-1

Contents

When you see one of these (*) look at the bottom of the page.

Ways to Use This Book

"Read some more!" is one of the most rewarding compliments a listener can give, for it reflects his feelings of wanting to repeat a pleasant experience.

WHY READ TO A CHILD?

Listening to a good story, well read, has many values for a child. It helps him learn to listen and thus increases his attention span. Listening to a good story also helps him develop his ability to retain a sequence of ideas. As he talks with you about a story he has heard, he gains experience in speaking and thus increases his vocabulary. And when your child snuggles down beside you to hear a story, an emotional closeness develops from his warm and personal interaction.

WHY READ BIBLE STORIES?

Our purpose in reading Bible stories to a child is to share with him the gospel of God's love and the meaning of that love for everyone. It's also a way of telling a child that WE highly value what God says to us in the Bible.

Reading and talking about Bible stories provide natural value-teaching situations. For example, in Story 2, Abraham was willing to share with Lot. This story offers a natural opportunity to talk about sharing with others.

STORY READING TIPS

1. Read daily. It's vital to establish and maintain a regular story time. The length of time isn't as important as its regularity. Some parents make story reading a bedtime ritual. Others include story time as a part of family times.

2. Read expressively. Let your voice reflect your enthusiasm for what you're reading so that your genuine interest in the story comes through. You can add variety and maintain the child's attention if you add "sound effects" to the words you read. For example, "There was cre-e-eaking and scra-a-aping and ri-i-ipping and twi-i-isting and cru-u-unching—"

Create excitement by speaking slightly faster. Whisper or pause briefly to add suspense. For example, "Run! Run!" Jonathan whispered, "Just get out of here! Quickly, before you get caught!"

Change the tone of your voice to identify and reflect the feelings of the Bible story characters. For instance, "Jesus!" he shouted, "Glory to God! I am healed!"

3. Read creatively. Young children, particularly, thrive on repetition. After your child has become quite familiar with a story, omit a word and let him "fill in the blank." Of

course, the word should be an important one, such as an action word or a person's name.

4. Follow the story with fun-to-do activities. Talk with your child about the Bible story to help clarify ideas presented in the story; to discuss how story characters may have felt; and to think of how we might have felt in a similar situation. You might let each listener ask another family member one question about the story.

Provide appropriate art materials for your children to use in drawing or painting a picture of his favorite part of the story.

Help your child learn to repeat with understanding the Bible verse given at the conclusion of each story. Talk together about the meaning of the verse. Ask, "What is another way to say this verse? . . ." Show your child where the verse is printed in the Bible. Let him underline with a red pencil the verse in his Bible (to help him locate it easily).

A child who is learning to use his Bible will be interested in finding the story for himself. Guide him in locating the story in relation to the Old and New Testaments; also in relation to adjacent books in the Bible.

Sing together the songs included in this book (see "Contents") as a part of your fun-to-do activities.

When God Made the World There Was No Litter

THE CREATION STORY

Do you know what litter is?

You find out soon enough when you go on a picnic.

The minute you get in the car your mother reminds you that there's a litter bag there in the back seat, and it's to USE, please. The next thing you know you've finished off your apple and you've rolled the window down a bit and tossed out the core–oops, you FORGOT.

After you get there, you get into your bathing suit and pull off your shoes and run for the beach and–oops–cans. But on you go, and–oops, watch that soda pop bottle and– OOPS be careful of that broken glass!

And later, after you've eaten your lunch, you DO remember that your rubbish goes in that big trash can over by the tree, but it's SUCH a lot of trouble to walk over to it and you're SURE you can hit it so you throw your trash but–

oops, you missed. So you start over to pick your trash up and—oops, your brother throws a frisbee your way and you run for it and the NEXT thing you know the trash is forgotten.

Do you think God made the world like that—all *trashy?*

He did NOT. He made the world absolutely CLEAN.

He didn't make the world any old way with paper cups and broken bottles on the beach. It had to be JUST RIGHT. He put everything in its place and everything STAYED right where He put it.

The first thing God made was the light. He just said, "Let there be light!"—and there WAS.

Then He separated the light from the darkness, so it would be light for awhile and then dark for awhile. And He called the light "day." And He called the darkness "night." But whether it was day or night, the air was pure and CLEAN, just the way God wanted it.

But God wasn't finished yet.

On the second day He said, "Let there be a sky." And there was! He stretched it out overhead like a curtain! It says so in the Bible.

So now the world had day and night and a sky and—oops.

It didn't have any land! Not one SPECK of land! It was completely covered with water!

So the third day God gathered the water together and separated it from the land. The earth quaked and groaned, and with great mighty HEAVES, the land pushed up through the water! Some of it high enough to make hills and GREAT mountains. Some of it only high enough to make valleys. And some of it just stayed flat. Now God had land! Mountains, huge high mountains! And hills and flat land and valleys! And the water? Oh there was LOTS of water

left. More than you can IMAGINE. Enough to make huge oceans and rivers and lakes. And enough left over to make little creeks and ponds. And He made them stay in their places, ESPECIALLY the huge oceans.

"This far you may go," He said, "and this far—but no farther," just as if the ocean were a baby. And the ocean has been obeying God ever since which is a jolly good thing for us, for when the ocean just BURPS we have a tidal wave. So now the world had day and night and a sky and water and land—and it was all CLEAN.

So now there was water AND LAND. And this is what God did with it. He spoke to the seeds that He had put in the land and He said, "GROW!"

And they did!

Some grew to make fruits and vegetables. And some grew just to make things beautiful—like trees and flowers.

On the fourth day God hung out the sun to shine by day. And He hung out the moon and the stars to shine by night. And He put each one in its own pathway—even every little star!

And He said, "Now stay in your own pathway, and remember, NO BUMPING." And the sun and the moon and every single star obeyed God. And each one stayed in its own pathway—way out in that vast space.

Do you know how big VAST is? It's just about as big as anything you can imagine—even bigger than that! Do you know that the sun is a million times bigger than the earth? And the nearest star that you can see is about twenty-four TRILLION miles away? And that there are probably 200 BILLION stars in just our own galaxy?* Did you think this

*That's the group of stars that are around our own earth.

14

is the only galaxy? No! There are THOUSANDS of galax-
ies, all hurtling through space at a TREMENDOUS speed
without bumping into each other!

What?

How many stars?

IMPOSSIBADRILLIONS!!!

Now let's get back to earth again. God wasn't finished
with it yet.

Now the earth had water and vegetables and fruit and
trees and flowers—oops.

There were no living creatures in it!

All that water—and no fishes! All that sky—and no birds!
All that land, and no animals!

So on the fifth day God made fishes and birds and
animals. First the fishes. ALL KINDS! You can't IMAG-
INE how many kinds, from the tiniest guppies to the biggest
SEA MONSTERS!

Then the birds. More kinds than you can dream of! From
tiny hummingbirds to huge PEACOCKS!

Then the animals. EVERY kind of animal you could
think of! From the tiniest mice to the biggest ELEPHANT!

God told the fishes to swim in the water. He told the birds
to fly in the air. And He told the animals to stay on the land.

Now God had everything! Land and water and sky and
sun and moon and—

Eagles and beagles

And wrens and hens

And sharks and larks

And guppies and puppies

AND FLAMINGOS!

Trees and bees—

And thrushes and rushes—

And ants and plants—
And frogs and bogs—
AND GERANIUMS!
Beaches and leeches—
And lakes and snakes—
And pears and bears—
And beets and leeks—
AND BUTTERFLIES!
Carrots and parrots—
And blossoms and possums—
And mountains and fountains—
And seas and bees—
AND JELLYFISH!
Owls and fowls—
And stars and Mars—
And turtles and myrtles—
And mice and lice—
And whales and snails—
And pines and limes—
And pigs and figs—
AND CROCODILES!
—OOPS!

There was still something missing! God had NOBODY to talk to!

Nobody He could LOVE and who would LOVE HIM BACK.

And that's when God did the most wonderful thing of all. HE CREATED MAN. "Let's make man in our own image," He said. It says so in the Bible. It tells us in the Bible that God created MAN and He named him ADAM.

And not only that.

He let Adam live in this wonderful world.

And not only that.

He let Adam be the BOSS over all fishes and birds and animals.

And not only that.

He let Adam NAME THEM ALL—EVERY SINGLE ONE.

So Adam named the ants and plants and quails and snails and sharks and larks and guppies and puppies—

(Oh dear. We can't go through all THAT again!)

ANYHOW—

Adam named them all. And he lived in this wonderful beautiful world God had made, and it was CLEAN. The water was clean, the beaches were clean, the forests were clean, the valleys were clean—

There were no paper cups that missed the trash cans, no broken glass, no soda pop bottles—and no apple cores thrown out of car windows!

"I want you to love me, Adam," God said, "and keep my beautiful world CLEAN."

And He's saying the same thing to us today. Not only to children—to GROWN-UPS too. There are some grown-ups who don't care enough to keep God's world clean.

What if things were turned around and children could scold grown-ups!

"Mrs. Messrubbish, ma'am, you really shouldn't have thrown that soda pop can on the ground. There's a trash can right over there."

Or, "Mr. Sloppygoppie, sir, you shouldn't leave all those paper plates and that garbage around. And DO put out your campfire!"

Or, "Miss Slobbuckle, ma'am, excuse me but you leave a

trail of dirt behind you wherever you go. Do pick some of it up."

Of course you probably couldn't do it, even if you were very polite about it. But you COULD set an example. You COULD go over and pick up the can or the paper cup or whatever and put it in the trash can yourself.

ANYHOW—

This world has been spinning around for many many years. And when God made it, IT WAS CLEAN.

Wouldn't it be wonderful, if after all these years, we could say today, "Here's God's beautiful world. And there are no paper cups lying around, or broken glass or soda pop cans—

AND NO LITTERBUGS!"

NOW FIND THIS STORY IN YOUR BIBLE

It's in Genesis, chapters 1 and 2:1-3.

A BIBLE VERSE TO LEARN

In the beginning God created the heaven and the earth (Gen. 1:1, *KJV*).

LET'S TALK TO GOD

Dear God, thank you for making such a beautiful world for us. Help us to remember to take care of it and keep it clean. In Jesus' name, Amen.

Sharing Is Here to Stay
ABRAHAM AND LOT

How do you feel about sharing? Do you always think you ought to have the best part of whatever has to be shared? Why? Because you're older? Or bigger and stronger?

Some people think they ought to have the best part because they're younger and smaller and weaker.

Well no matter how you feel about it, you'd better get used to the idea of sharing because sharing has been around for a long long time.

I'm going to tell you a story about a man way back in Bible times who learned a lesson about sharing. His name was Abraham and he lived in the city of Ur.

Now the city of Ur was way off in the desert and it had temples and libraries and schools and houses, gleaming white in the sun—it was a BEAUTIFUL city.

It was full of splashing fountains.

And it had palm trees that clattered and chattered in the wind.

And the people lived in comfortable two-story houses made of brick and plaster.

And there was plenty of room for all the mothers and fathers and children and servants—room for everybody.

And the children went to school and learned to read and write and do arithmetic and they laughed at their play and the babies squealed and squrgled.

Now Abraham was rich. He had lots of flocks and herds and goats and cattle and camels and donkeys—and he had gold and silver too. He had a father whose name was Terah. And he had a wife whose name was Sarah. And he had a nephew whose name was Lot. And it's Abraham and Lot who had to learn about sharing. And it all came about because God asked Abraham to leave the beautiful city of Ur and go to another land. And God said HE would show Abraham the way.

Yes sir—Abraham used to go outside at night and watch the stars. And one night while he was watching the stars, God spoke to him. "Abraham," God said, "I want you to get out of this city and go to another land. And I will show you the way." Just like that!

And do you know what? Abraham actually DID it!

Yes sir, Abraham and his family got to work and they packed rugs and jugs and blankets and tents and all kinds of food. And they loaded them on camels and donkeys. And they said good-bye to all their aunts and uncles and cousins and nephews and nieces and friends—all except one nephew.

And that was Lot.

Abraham decided to take him along.

So off they went, across the hot sunny desert. Some of them rode. Some of them walked alongside. Some of them kept the cattle and sheep together. And some of them ran after the children so they wouldn't wander off and get lost.

And at night there were no motels where they could stop and sleep. No siree. They had to pitch their tents and build a fire and cook their own supper and sleep on rugs on the ground. But before they went to sleep they always thanked God for watching over them.

And after everybody was asleep, Abraham went out under the stars and talked to God.

There were no signposts saying "NEW COUNTRY—200 MILES." And there were no road maps. And there was no highway patrol to flag down and ask which way to go. But Abraham wasn't worried. He had better directions than any highway patrolman could have given him, for GOD was telling him which way to go.

And finally—

God said to Abraham—

"This is IT."

Oh what a beautiful place it was! Just like a picture! There were rolling hills and valleys, with grass, like a green velvet carpet. And trees and flowers and little brooks running down from the hills.

All this! It looked like all the room in the world for Abraham and his family and Lot and his family to live in.

Well, the very FIRST thing they did was to pile up a lot of stones and make an altar. And Abraham thanked God for keeping them all safe. And then they unpacked all their pots and pans and rugs and jugs and blankets and tents. And they settled down and began to live.

And then things began to happen!

Their flocks and herds began to get bigger! Their cows had calves and their sheep had lambs and their dogs had puppies and their cats had kittens and their donkeys had little donklettes and their camels had little camelettes.

But that was all right.

They had PLENTY of grass for all their animals to eat.

But then their cows had more calves and their sheep had more lambs and their donkeys had more little donklettes and their camels had more camelettes and—

But that was all right.

There was ALMOST enough pasture land for all of them.

But then their herds of cattle and sheep got BIGGER AND BIGGER AND BIGGER, and—

You guessed it.

There was no longer enough room for all of them.

When Abraham's servants took their cattle and sheep to a pasture to eat, LOT'S cattle were there.

And when Lot's servants took THEIR cattle to a pasture to eat, ABRAHAM'S cattle were there.

And it wasn't long before they were all mixed up.

They had SCRAMBLED flocks and herds.

And nobody knew which was WHOSE.

"This is OUR spot!" Lot's servants would bellow.

"No it is NOT. This is OUR spot," Abraham's servants would roar.

And so they bellowed and roared at each other until finally Abraham heard about it. And THIS is when the little problem of SHARING came up.

Now Abraham already knew that land was HIS. And it WAS. God had given it to HIM. But nonetheless he took Lot up on a high hill where they could look down on all the land.

And Abraham said, "Lot—let's not quarrel. And let's not let our servants quarrel. There's enough land for both of us. Look at it! As far as you can see! We can SHARE it! I'll take one part and you take another."

Now Abraham COULD have said, "I'll take the BEST part. Because God gave it to me in the first place. Besides I'm bigger than you and I'm older than you. And that says I should have the best part."

Instead of that he said, "Lot, YOU choose the part YOU want. And I'll take what's left over."

WOW!

And Lot could have been very polite and said, "No Uncle Abraham, YOU are the one God gave it to in the first place. Besides you're OLDER than me."

But he didn't.

Do you know what Lot did instead?

He looked at one side where the grass was green and beautiful, with a big RIVER running through it. And he looked at the other side. There wasn't much grass. And there was no river. And he pointed to the BEST part. And he said, "Uncle Abraham. I'll take THAT part."

Oh-oh, Lot—you just blew it!

Well, Lot took his family and his servants and his cattle and his sheep and he moved down into the very best part of the land!And he settled down there in the valley to live.

And Abraham and Sarah and his family and his servants and his cattle and his sheep took the other part.

And Abraham didn't go to bed and pull the blankets up over his head and SULK, either. Even though he was stuck with the worst part.

Instead he built an altar. And he thanked God. Because Abraham knew he didn't have to fight for his rights or watch out for himself and take the best part. He knew that GOD was watching out for him.

And that's what counted.

And God DID watch out for Abraham. He made him richer and more powerful and gave him a long life—

But best of all—

God gave Abraham and his wife Sarah the one thing they wanted more than anything else in the world!

God gave them a son!

A squirggling baby boy!

He was fat and dimpled and beautiful. They named him Isaac and that meant laughter! And Isaac was the happiest boy in the world!

Well you might as well get used to the idea of sharing, because it's been around for a long long time.

And do you know what?

As long as the world is turning and as long as God is in heaven—sharing is here to stay.

NOW FIND THIS STORY IN YOUR BIBLE

It's in Genesis, chapters 13 and 15.

A BIBLE VERSE TO LEARN

Do not merely look out for your own personal interests, but also for the interests of others (Phil. 2:4, *NASB*).

LET'S TALK TO GOD

Dear God, it isn't very easy to choose the next best and give somebody else the best. But we know that you want us to share. Help us to want to please you. In Jesus' name, Amen.

You Shouldn't Quarrel—But If You Do—

JOSEPH AND HIS BROTHERS

Do you have brothers and sisters? How do you get along with them? Are you always kind to each other? Or do you quarrel sometimes?

"Mom gave you the biggest piece!"

"She did not!"

"Yes she did too!"

"Well I'm smarter than you are."

"You are not."

"I am so."

"You're bragging."

"Am not."

"Are too! Mom, he's bragging."

"I am NOT."

♪ "You ARE. You're a brag, you're a brag, I think you're a great big drag!"

Wooops, wait a minute.

I want to tell you a story about a boy who lived way back in Bible times. His name was Joseph—and did HE ever have a lot of brothers! He had ten BIG brothers and one BABY brother. And when they all sat around the breakfast table and passed the barley cakes and honey, believe me it was pretty noisy.

Joseph's father was very rich. He had sheep and goats and donkeys and camels—more of them than you could count. And Joseph helped his father and his brothers watch the sheep and the cattle. And he hunted and he rode the donkeys. And he stopped sometimes to tickle his baby brother's feet. But he never tickled his older brothers' feet. In fact there was NOTHING about Joseph that tickled his older brothers.

And did THEY quarrel! They quarreled about a lot of things. There was the time Joseph's father gave him a beautiful coat. And when Joseph scampered off to show the coat to his brothers, THEY didn't think it was beautiful. They scowled and scuffed the ground with their feet and they mumbled—mumblmumblmumbl—

They were angry.

And they were jealous.

And then there was the time that Joseph had those dreams. Did they ever quarrel over THEM! Phew!

"D'you know what?" Joseph said. "I had the most amazing dream last night." And he reached for the barley cakes. "In my dream we were all tying up grain in bundles. And MY bundle stood up straight. But YOUR bundles— may I have some honey?—YOUR BUNDLES—"

"And our bundles?" his brothers grumbled. "What did our bundles do?"

Joseph dove into his barley cakes. "Your bundles," he said, "bowed down to MY bundle."

Phew! Did THAT ever start a quarrel.

"Do you think you're going to be a KING or something?" they bellowed, "And rule over us?" And they tackled their barley cakes with howls and growls.

Well, sir, that dream was bad enough, but when the SECOND dream came along—Phew!

"I had another dream," he said. "Wait'll you hear THIS one. This time it was stars."

Stars! They all stopped chewing their barley cakes and stared at him.

"Yep, stars," he said happily. "Eleven of them. And that's not all. The SUN bowed down to me. And the MOON too."

Well this time even Joseph's father thought this was "a bit much." He shot Joseph one of those "Enough!" looks. "Come come, Joseph," he said. "If the eleven stars are supposed to be your brothers—"

Joseph shrugged.

"Then the sun and the moon are supposed to be your father and mother! So your father and mother are going to bow down to you too?"

"Well if you think WE'RE going to bow down to you," his brothers scoffed, "forget it! No way!" They were very VERY angry.

After that things didn't go well, they didn't go well at all. "Here comes the dreamer," Joseph's brothers would say when they saw him coming, and "There goes the dreamer," they'd say when he walked away.

And then the day came when Joseph probably wished he

had stuck to eating his barley cakes instead of telling his brothers about those dreams.

For something DREADFUL happened.

It happened because Joseph's brothers were far away where they'd gone to find pasture for their sheep. And Joseph's father sent him to go see if they were all right. And Joseph put on the beautiful coat his father had given him and started on the long long trek to find his brothers. He didn't know it, but when he found them, something was going to happen that would change his whole life.

When his brothers saw him coming in the distance, the first thing they saw were the beautiful colors in that coat. And all their old jealousy came back over them like a tidal wave.

"Well if it isn't the dreamer," they said, and when they thought about those dreams they got angry all over again. "Let's throw him in a pit," they said, "and forget him." And they watched him coming closer.

"Father sent me—" Joseph started—and that was as far as he got.

They GRABBED him.

And they TORE OFF HIS COAT.

And they DRAGGED HIM OVER TO THE PIT.

And they PUSHED—HIM—IN!

"Ohhhhhhhh," Joseph thought, "ANYTHING could happen now."

And something did.

Joseph's brothers got an idea that changed Joseph's whole life.

It happened when the brothers saw something coming way off in the distance. First it was just a speck. But as it came closer they saw that it was—

A caravan of merchants with camels and donkeys loaded with goods to sell in Egypt!

"Let's sell JOSEPH," they said, "and we'll never have to see him again!" Now the caravan was close enough to hear the camel bells. Then it came to a halt and the bells stopped ringing.

"Want to buy a boy?" the brothers called out.

And down in his pit, Joseph went ULP.

"He'll make a good slave!" they said. And some of them reached down and pulled Joseph out of the pit.

"We sure do!" the merchants called back.

And Joseph went GULP.

"Come along, boy," the merchants said, pulling him toward the caravan.

And Joseph thought HELP.

But it was no use. Joseph was dragged off to Egypt far far away. His brothers had sold him as if he were a bundle of grain or a batch of barley cakes.

And then they went home and told their father that Joseph was dead. "That's the end of the dreamer," they thought.

But was it?

Let's see what happened.

Joseph was sold as a slave to a man named Potiphar, and went to live in his beautiful house. And then—and THEN—

Things began to happen! Some of the things were good. And some of the things were bad.

First, Joseph was so good and so honest that Potiphar made him master over all the slaves in his house!

Oh joy!

But then—Potiphar's wife told Potiphar that Joseph had

done something very wicked and Potiphar put Joseph in PRISON.

Oh gloom.

But then—While he was in prison he met another prisoner who was the butler to the GREAT PHARAOH OF EGYPT.* And this prisoner had a strange dream and told Joseph about it, and Joseph told him what the dream meant! And it meant, of all things, that the butler would be free from prison. And it happened just as Joseph said it would! And the butler promised Joseph that he would ask the king to let Joseph out of prison!

Oh joy!

But THEN—The months went by—

And TWO WHOLE YEARS WENT BY—

And nothing happened. The butler had forgotten his promise.

Oh gloom.

But THEN—The KING had a dream. And nobody could tell him what it meant. And then the butler remembered HIS dream. And he also remembered his promise! And he told the king that Joseph could tell him what his dream meant. And the king sent for Joseph to come to the palace!

Oh joy!

And Joseph DID tell the king what his dream meant. It meant that in a few years there would be a famine in the land because nothing would grow.

And the people wouldn't have any food.

And that they had better store up food NOW so they'd have enough when it happened.

*The King of Egypt

34

And the king told Joseph that he could be—that he could be—

Was it Oh joy?

Or Oh gloom?

Well we'll find out about that in a minute. IN THE MEANTIME—

The famine came as Joseph had said it would, and it was all over the land. It was even back where Joseph's brothers and his father lived. The ground dried up. Nothing would grow. The cattle had no grass to eat. And the people had no food.

"Whatever shall we do?" Joseph's brothers cried.

"There's only one thing we CAN do," said Joseph's father. "You will have to go to Egypt and buy some grain. In Egypt they've been storing up grain for years. They have great storehouses and barns LOADED with grain. I'll stay home with your youngest brother."

So Joseph's brothers took donkeys and made the long trek into Egypt. And when they got there, and got to one of the huge storehouses, who was selling the grain but the head man—the great Egyptian ruler next to the king himself! They all bowed down before him.

And did he ever look STERN.

And were they ever SCARED.

And he gave them a hard time, too! "You are SPIES!" he said, and he had them all put in prison! Then he told them they could all go home IF they left one of the brothers behind. Oh, he was stern!

He asked them a lot of questions.

They told him they had an old father and a younger brother at home.

And THEN he told them they'd better come BACK with the youngest brother—or ELSE!

Well, they went home in fear and trembling and got their youngest brother and went back to Egypt again, more frightened than ever. And oh, did they EVER have their ups and downs!

First he asked them all about their family.

Then he let them go home.

Then he made them come back.

Then he invited them to his palace for dinner.

Then he let them go home again.

Then he made them come back.

He seemed to change his mind every time they turned around.

They didn't know whether they were coming or going!

Then he invited them back to his palace again. And they all bowed down before him. And then—and then—AND THEN—

"Look at me," said the great ruler of Egypt next to the king.

They stared at him, trembling.

"Don't you know me?" he said.

They didn't know how to answer. Whatever was he up to now?

Then they saw—they saw—

They saw that he had tears in his eyes!!?!!

He looked back at them eyeball to eyeball. "I am your brother Joseph," he said.

What?

What?

WHAT?

This was JOSEPH?

Their brother whom they had sold as a SLAVE?!??

Yes indeed it was. For THAT was what the king had told Joseph he could be. He had told Joseph that he could be—that he could be—

The chief ruler of Egypt next to the king himself!!!

Now Joseph could have said, "You quarreled with me and you sold me as a slave and now it's my turn to get even."

Do you suppose he did? *Do you suppose he did?*

No.

Instead—he forgave them! "Don't be afraid of me," he said, "and don't be sorry you sold me. God has made me chief ruler of Egypt next to the king himself, so I could provide you with food."

And then he hugged them.

And the tears ran down his face.

And splashed on their heads.

Oh joy!

It was almost too good to believe!

And they laughed and cried and thanked God that they were all safe. And they sent for their old father—

And their youngest brother—

And they all lived in Egypt, all together again!

Do you have brothers and sisters? How do you get along with them? Are you always kind to each other? Or do you quarrel sometimes? And if you do—

If you DO—

Do you forgive each other?

NOW FIND THIS STORY IN YOUR BIBLE

It's in Genesis, chapters 37 and 39:1 to 45:15.

38

A BIBLE VERSE TO LEARN

And be ye kind one to another, tenderhearted, forgiving one another, even as God for Christ's sake hath forgiven you (Eph. 4:32, *KJV*).

LET'S TALK TO GOD

Dear God, thank you for taking care of us as you did Joseph. Help us to be kind to our family and our friends. And if others do something to us that we don't like, help us to forgive them. In Jesus name, Amen.

Should You Thank God— Some of the Time?

MOSES LEAVES EGYPT

Do you thank God for His goodness to you?

"Sure, always."

Always?

"Well—almost always."

Awwww, come on. Think again.

"Well—sometimes I do."

I'm sure you do.

But do you know that there are some people who would have to say "Never"?

"Aw NO—that's AWFUL."

Well, there are. There are some people who NEVER thank God for ANYTHING.

But some of us thank Him MOST of the time.

And some of us thank Him SOME of the time.

This is a story about some people who thanked Him SOME of the time.

They were God's people—way back in Bible times.

They were called Hebrews way back then, and they were

40

SLAVES to a king in Egypt. He was called the Pharaoh, and was HE ever a rascal! He made the Hebrews work from sunup to sundown, making bricks. And when they didn't make enough bricks in a day, they were whipped.

But God had not forgotten them.

No sir. He gave them a LEADER.

And his name was Moses.

And God said to Moses, "Go to the Pharaoh and tell him to let my people go free. And don't be afraid. I'll be with you."

And Moses did.

He stood right up to the Pharaoh, eyeball to eyeball, and he said, "Oh Pharaoh—God says to let these people go. Let them go for just three days so they can worship Him in the wilderness."

Well sir, the Pharaoh leaned forward on his throne and his voice was like a thunderclap. "And who is GOD that I should let these people go?"

"He is the God of the Hebrews," Moses said. "And He has spoken to me. Let us go, we pray you."

"The answer is NO!" Pharaoh bellowed. "I am the PHARAOH, and I answer to no one! These people are my slaves. Why do you keep them from doing their work? If they don't have enough to keep them busy I'll give them MORE!"

And he did.

He made them work harder than ever before. And when they cried out in complaint, he said, "You are IDLE, you are IDLE. It is because you are IDLE that you ask to go on journeys in the wilderness to worship your God. Work harder! Work harder! Then you'll have no time for journeys!"

Then Moses fired his bombshell. "Let us go," he warned, "or God will PUNISH you!"

"I don't believe it," thought Pharaoh. And that was the biggest mistake he ever made in his life.

For there followed a series of punishments so strange and so dreadful that there has never been anything like them since, in all the world.

First—

The great river Nile that flowed through Egypt and watered all the gardens—TURNED TO BLOOD!

And the fish died.

And the people had no water.

Then—

FROGS! God sent frogs—millions of them. They were all over the country and in the cities—

Frogs in the gardens—
   Frogs in the streets—
      Frogs in the houses—
         Frogs in the living rooms—
         Frogs in the kitchens—
            Frogs in the PALACE—
               Frogs on the Pharaoh's table—
               Frogs in the Pharaoh's bed—
                  Frogs in the Pharaoh's BED?!???!!?

And then—

FLIES! Horrible stinging flies!

Flies in the houses—
   Flies in the kitchens—
      Flies in the palace—
         Flies in the Pharaoh's bed—
            Flies in the Pharaoh's BED???!?!??

"Wait!" bellowed Pharaoh. "I'll give you all a few days off and you can worship your God right here!"

"No," said Moses. "Out of the country. You must let us go out of the country. That's the way God wants it."

But in spite of all the punishment, Pharaoh was still stubborn.

"No!" he shouted. He wasn't finished yet.

But neither was God.

Then—DISEASE!

It killed most of their cattle—their oxen, their sheep—

Then—HAIL! Huge chunks of hail like baseballs; it beat down what crops were left in the field. And it killed off the rest of the cattle.

"WAIT!" Pharaoh cried. "Stop it, STOP IT! You may go! But leave your women and children behind! And all your cattle!"*

"No," said Moses, "We ALL go."

"No—you can't do that!" Pharaoh shouted, "No! NO!" He wasn't finished yet.

But neither was God.

Then—LOCUSTS! They swarmed all over everything. They came like a great army. Nothing could stop them!

Locusts in the houses

Locusts in the PALACE—

Locusts in the Pharaoh's bed—

Locusts in the Pharaoh's BED??!?!

"WAIT!" screamed Pharaoh. "Stop it, STOP IT! You may go! Take your women and children too! But leave your CATTLE behind!"

"No," said Moses.

*None of these punishments affected the Hebrews; it was only the Egyptians who lost their crops and cattle.

44

"Then MY answer is also NO!" Pharaoh shouted again, louder this time. He wasn't finished yet.

But neither was God.

"Then tonight about midnight," Moses said quietly. "ALL the firstborn Egyptian children will die. And don't say God didn't warn you."

Well, the Pharaoh had his warning and he had his chance to change his mind. But he wouldn't listen.

And then—and THEN—

God said to Moses, "The time has come. You shall lead these people out of Egypt this very night."

Then Moses told the people what they were supposed to do.

"Gather all your things—"

"Yes, Moses," the people said.

"Prepare a supper. Not any old supper. A SPECIAL supper. Roast lamb! And bread! And herbs! And all cooked in a SPECIAL way." And Moses told them just how to do it—the way God had said they should.

"Yes, Moses."

"And wait for the signal."

Phew! Was THIS ever going to be exciting!

So the people did everything Moses told them to do.

And then they waited.

Quietly.

Until it was midnight!

Then suddenly—

A cry went up through the air.

The firstborn child in every Egyptian family was dead!*

The Pharaoh sent for Moses.

*The Pharaoh could have prevented this, if he had obeyed!

"Go!" he cried, "ALL of you! Go, go GO! Get out of Egypt and NEVER COME BACK!"

So Moses went back to the people. "Now," he said. "The time has come. This very night we shall leave Egypt."

And they did. The families tumbled out of their houses. Fathers and mothers and children and grandfathers and grandmothers and uncles and aunts and cousins. With goats and sheep and wagons and carts and donkeys and bundles—and gold and silver and jewelry too!* Thousands of them. Thousands and thousands!

And that very night they left Egypt to go through a great wilderness, toward a wonderful land that God had promised them.**

It was while they were going through this wilderness that the "Thank you" business came in. And, sad to say, the Hebrews did not thank God all the time. They didn't even thank Him MOST of the time. They thanked Him only SOME of the time.

When they found water to drink, they thanked Him.

When they ran out of water, they GRUMBLED.

When God sent thousands and thousands of birds, called quail, flying so low they could reach right up with their hands and catch them to eat, they thanked Him.

But when they ran out of quail, they grumbled.

When God sent them food dropped right from the sky, they thanked Him and called the food "manna."***

But when they got tired of the manna, they grumbled and

*The Egyptians were so glad to get rid of them, they gave them gold and silver and jewelry to hasten them on their way!
**How they got there is a long l-o-n-g story. You can read all about it in *Ethel Barrett Tells Bible Stories To Children, Volume 2.*
***Which means "What is it?"

mumbled. They were the mumbliest grumbliest people you could ever imagine.

But they did remember to thank God at least SOME of the time.

And ONE of those times was the happiest and most exciting adventure they ever had!

It was the time Moses told them God wanted them to build Him a church!

What? A church in the WILDERNESS?

Yes. A TENT church! To be made in such a way that they could take it all apart when they traveled and carry it right along with them!

"And God wants you to bring your gifts to build it," Moses said. "He told me all the things we would need. Are you willing? God wants gifts only from people who are WILLING."

Were they ever WILLING! They sure were!

They ran to their tents and brought out their gifts—gold and silver and rings and bracelets and earrings and pins. And rams' skins and badgers' skins and goats' skins and red cloth and blue cloth and purple cloth—

"Stop!" Moses cried. "Don't bring any more! You've brought so many gifts we can't use them all up!"

And so everybody got busy.

The workmen cut boards from acacia trees. They melted the jewelry down to big pots of gold and silver and brass. They covered the boards with gold and made hooks of silver and bowls of brass and a golden candlestick and a table and an altar and beautiful curtains—

Then they fastened the golden boards together—

They hung the beautiful curtains over the top—

They put goats' hair curtains over the curtains—
And rams' skins over the goats' hair—
And badgers' skins over EVERYTHING so the rain wouldn't get in.

Then they put the special golden furniture inside—
And the rest of the curtains—
—Until at last the beautiful Tabernacle was finally finished.

And they all gathered around it. And they began to PRAISE GOD. They praised Him with singing. They praised Him by praying. And they praised Him by THANKING Him.

They thanked Him for everything they could think of. They had a long list of things to thank Him for, but most of all, they thanked Him for delivering them out of Egypt!

And always and forever more, whenever they thanked Him, their escape from Egypt was at the top of the list!

Do you thank God for His goodness to you?
Some of us thank him SOME of the time.
Some of us thank Him MOST of the time.
But He would like us to thank Him ALL of the time.

NOW FIND THIS STORY IN YOUR BIBLE

It's in Exodus 35:4 to chapter 36 and 39:27-43 and 40:17-38.

A BIBLE VERSE TO LEARN

This Bible verse tells us ways to praise God.
Sing to the Lord, bless His name; proclaim good tidings of His salvation from day to day (Ps. 96:2, *NASB*).

LET'S TALK TO GOD

Dear God, thank you for protecting us. Thank you for giving us food to eat and clothes to wear. Thank you for our churches. We're sorry we don't always remember to thank you for the things you do for us. In Jesus' name, Amen.

What Should a Best Friend Be Like?

DAVID AND JONATHAN

Did you ever have a best friend? You know, the kind when you both took vows and promised to be best friends forever?

"I hereby solemnly promise to be your best friend forever and ever. And nothing shall ever part us no matter what happens."

Ever do that?

What do you think a best friend ought to be like?

"Well—I'd want him to be true and kind and—well, I wouldn't want him to be jealous of me, that's for sure. And I'd want him to help me out if I ever got in trouble. THAT'S for sure. And I'd sure want him to be friendly. THAT'S for sure."

Well, this is a story about two boys who were best friends, way back in Bible times.

One of them was David. And of course EVERYBODY knows about David. He was the boy who put a stone in his

51

slingshot, wound up for the pitch and—hurled it through the air and—KILLED A GIANT. And after that he was taken to the palace of the great King Saul. And oh how the people cheered and shouted and fussed over David because he had killed that giant.

That was the happy part. But THEN—

King Saul became JEALOUS. That was the SAD part.

But there was another happy part.

For while David was at King Saul's palace, he met Jonathan.

And Jonathan was King Saul's SON.

He was a PRINCE.

And David and Jonathan became best friends. Their friendship just busted out all over, right on the spot. The Bible tells us that David and Jonathan loved each other on sight.

And Jonathan the PRINCE gave David the SHEPHERD boy his robe and his sword and his bow and his belt! That meant he loved David for sure. And those two boys vowed to be best friends forever and no matter what happened.

Well the years went by, and those years were pretty bumpy—David and Jonathan had their ups and downs.

One week King Saul would be kind to David. That would be an UP.

And the next week he'd chase him out of the palace and tell him to never come back. That would be a DOWN.

Well David knew that King Saul was jealous. But he didn't know that King Saul was planning to have him—

MURDERED.

Yes!

King Saul called some of his officials together, and his son Jonathan too—and he glowered and scowled and tugged

at his beard. "I want to have David killed," he said.

Now including Jonathan in that meeting was a big mistake. For Jonathan was not about to let his best friend get killed.

So the very first chance he had, he got ahold of David.

"Listen David," he said, "listen HARD. Don't interrupt me. Don't say a word. And don't ask me any questions. I have to talk fast."

David nodded.

"Tomorrow morning," Jonathan said, "find a hiding place out in the fields. I'll ask my father to take a walk with me out there. And I'll talk to him about you. Then I'll tell you everything he says."

David started to say something but Jonathan pushed him on his way. "Run! Run!" Jonathan whispered. "Just get out of here! Quickly, before you get caught!"

Well, Saul did agree to go for a walk with Jonathan, and Jonathan tried to reason with him.

"Father," Jonathan pleaded, "David has never harmed you. He's done you nothing but good. You know that."

King Saul just scowled.

"Father, have you forgotten how he killed the giant? And God helped us win the battle because of it."

King Saul scowled harder.

Jonathan tried again. "Father, there's no reason why you should want him killed. Please!"

King Saul stopped a minute and tugged at his beard again. "All right, son," he said finally. "All right. I promise. I won't have David killed. I promise."

Jonathan sighed with relief. His best friend wouldn't be killed!

King Saul turned and started back to the palace. "I want to stay here and think for awhile, Father," Jonathan said. "I'll come back later." And King Saul started back alone.

Jonathan waited until he was out of sight.

Then—

"Psssst. David!" he whispered. "You can come out now!"

And David crawled out from behind a pile of rocks. "David, everything's all right," Jonathan said. "My father promised me he wouldn't have you killed."

"Are you sure?"

"Yes! He PROMISED me! You can come back with me now. There's nothing to be afraid of. Everything's going to be ALL RIGHT!"

Oh joy!

And David did go back to live in the palace and everything was all right—

For awhile.

And then King Saul began to get jealous again.

And one day things were UP.

And the next day things were DOWN.

And the next day things were UP.

And the next day things were DOWN.

Then one day things went DOWN and they didn't go back UP again.

They just went down
down
down
down
down—

"Jonathan," David finally said, "I KNOW your father is going to kill me."

Jonathan sighed.

This time he was afraid his best friend David was right.

"I'll try to find out," he said. "But you must stay in hiding. But how will I let you know?"

"We could use our old hideout," David said.

"Right," said Jonathan. "Be at the hideout where you were before, out by the stone pile. And I'll come out for some target-practice with my bow and arrows."

"Yes," David said, listening hard.

"And I'll bring a boy with me."

David listened harder.

"And I'll shoot three arrows as if I were shooting at a target. Do you get that?"

"I get that."

"Now," Jonathan went on, "if I shoot them in FRONT of the stone pile I'll send the boy to bring them back. And I'll shout LOUD so you'll be sure to hear. I'll shout 'They're on THIS side!' And that will mean that everything is all right. BUT—"

David listened HARDER.

"If I shoot them PAST the stone pile, I'll shout at the boy "Go farther, Go FARTHER—the arrows are still up ahead of you! And that will mean—"

David shook his head sadly. "I know," he said. "That will mean I'll have to run away."

"Yes David," said Jonathan. "It means you run for your life."

And they took ahold of each others' hands and they vowed to be friends forever, no matter what happened.

Well—

From there on out, the news was all bad. For King Saul was not just a little bit angry. He wasn't even VERY angry. HE WAS FURIOUS!

"AUUUUUUUUGH!" he shouted. "Go find that good-for-nothing David and bring him here so I can kill him! GO FIND HIMMMMMM!!!"

It was a sad day.

Jonathan took a servant boy with him and went off to practice shooting his arrows. And he headed straight for the field where the hideout was.

"All right, start running," he told the servant boy. And he put his arrow in his bow and he whuuuuuuped it through the air.

"Now!" he called after the boy. "Here comes one! Watch it!" The boy ran after it.

And then Jonathan put another arrow in his bow. He took a deep breath. Then he pulled the string waaaay back and he shot the arrow—whuuuuuuupt!—straight and true—right over the boy's head—and PAST THE STONE PILE.

That was the signal.

And THEN—As the boy got up to the FIRST arrow that had been shot, Jonathan shouted, "No—go on, go ON! I shot one up ahead of you! IT'S WAY UP AHEAD OF YOU!!!"

Jonathan wondered.

Did David get it?

Did he understand?

Jonathan yelled again, "HURRY—DON'T WAIT!!!" And the boy went PAST the pile of rocks.

And he picked up the arrow.

And then he came back.

"All right. You can go back to the palace now," Jonathan said to the boy. "I don't want to practice any more."

The boy went on his way. But Jonathan never stopped watching that pile of rocks.

And in a minute—

Out scrambled David.

And Jonathan and David—the two best friends—stood there and looked at each other for a minute. This was the saddest day in all their lives. They walked toward each other, those two best friends. And they put their hands on each other's shoulders. And the tears ran down their cheeks.

"Remember David," Jonathan said, "we've given ourselves to God forever. And He's promised that He will take care of us."

"Promise me, Jonathan," David said, "we'll always be best friends?"

"We'll always be best friends," said Jonathan, "forever."

And do you know what?

They WERE best friends for all the rest of their lives.

What did you say you wanted your best friend to be like? True and kind and friendly and not jealous?

Well that's what you'd want your FRIEND to be like. NOW.

Do you think that YOU could be that kind of a person too? Well if you can—if you CAN—you'll have—not only a BEST friend—you'll have MORE friends than you'll be able to count!

NOW FIND THIS STORY IN YOUR BIBLE

It's in 1 Samuel 18:1-4 and 19:1-7 and chapter 20.

A BIBLE VERSE TO LEARN

And so, as those who have been chosen of God, holy and

beloved, put on a heart of compassion, kindness, humility, gentleness and patience (Col. 3:12, *NASB*).

LET'S TALK TO GOD

Dear God, thank you for my best friends. Help me to always be a faithful, true and kind best friend. In Jesus' name, Amen.

Some Tests Are Hard to Pass—Unless!

DANIEL IN THE LION'S DEN

Suppose—just suppose that you could go to a far away land and live in a palace. And you could have anything you wanted—beautiful clothes—all kinds of the best food—anything money could buy, no matter how much it cost.

How do you like that idea?

Oh.

There's one little hitch.

While you lived in that palace and had all those wonderful things, you would ALSO have to do everything the other people in the palace did, from the king right down to the people who worked in the kitchen. And some of the things they did were NO-NO'S. So if you did them, you would be disobeying God.

NOW how do you like that idea?

Well this actually happened to the boy in our story. His name was Daniel and a fine strapping lad he was—strong and healthy and very very smart.

He lived in the city of Jerusalem. And he went off to the far away city of Babylon. Only he didn't go there on a vacation. No—the city of Jerusalem had been CONQUERED by the king of Babylon, and Daniel was carried off to Babylon as a CAPTIVE.

And he wound up in the king's palace!

And this is how it happened.

"Send me some boys," the king had said. "I want them to be trained, to have the finest of educations, so I can use them when they get to be men to help me rule my kingdom. And I want them to be strapping lads, strong and healthy and very very smart."

And who was one of the boys to be chosen?

You guessed it.

Daniel.

He was taken to the palace along with some of his friends. And they had beautiful clothes, the finest education— ANYTHING THEY WANTED.

But here was the hitch.

The people in Babylon worshiped idols. Gold idols, silver idols, wooden idols—ALL KINDS OF IDOLS.

And they PRAYED to these idols. And they sacrificed some of their FOOD to these idols.

And Daniel and his friends had to eat the king's food. And drink the king's wine.

And Daniel had to decide whether to eat the king's food and drink the king's wine—

Or obey God!

That was quite a test. What? Be brave enough to go to the

counsellor in charge of food and tell him you couldn't eat the king's food, and couldn't you please have something else?

Phew!

But that's EXACTLY what Daniel did.

"What?!?" said the counselor. "I can't do this. You won't be merry like the others. You'll be pale.

"And you'll be SAD.

"And do you know what the king will do to me? Off with my HEAD!" And he drew his finger across his throat and rolled his eyes to show what he meant.

"But sir," Daniel blurted out, "try us. Just TRY us. Just give us vegetables and herbs to eat and water to drink instead of meat and wine."

"Vegetables?" exploded the counselor, "and water?"

"Just for ten days, sir," Daniel said. "And after ten days compare us with the other boys. See how we LOOK. See how we FEEL."

The counselor mopped his brow, thinking of his head being lopped off and rolling into a basket. He was sweating.

"All right," he said finally. "But only for ten days." And he heaved a big sigh.

And so it was. The other lads ate the king's food and drank wine with their meals. And Daniel and his friends ate their vegetables and herbs and drank water.

And at the end of ten days—

"Well, Daniel?" the counselor said.

"Well, sir?" said Daniel. "And how do we look?"

The counselor looked at Daniel, frowning. Then slowly his frown turned into a GRIN. "You look better. And so do your friends. And you all look HAPPIER than the others!"

"Yes sir."

"And HEALTHIER."

"Yes sir."

"And SMARTER."

"Yes sir," Daniel said modestly. "It is the wisdom of God."

"In fact," said the counselor, "you look G-R-E-A-A-A-T-T!"

Well, it was true. God gave Daniel and his friends wisdom and understanding and skill. They breezed through their training with no trouble at all. And they were found to be TEN TIMES BETTER than all the wise men of that day!

And they were put on the king's regular staff of advisors!

And so the years went on. And Daniel grew to be a V.I.P.* And as he got placed in higher and higher positions of authority, his tests grew harder and harder.

And HARDER.

And when Babylon changed kings and the new king made Daniel the head over ALL THE GOVERNORS IN THE KINGDOM—the other governors got jealous.

And THAT'S when Daniel's biggest test came.

The jealous governors went to the king. "Oh king," they said, "we want everybody to know who is the boss around here. And to show them, we'd like to make a law saying that no man in your kingdom can pray to any other god, or ask a favor of any man—except YOU!"

The king nodded, pleased.

"And," the governors went on, "anybody who DOES will be THROWN INTO THE LIONS' DEN!!!"

"Great idea!" said the king. "Go to it!"

AND THEY DID!

"GOTCHA, Daniel," the governors thought. For they

*Very important person!

65

knew that he would pray to God, NO MATTER WHAT! And they thought again, "GOTCHA!"

Then Daniel heard about it.

What?

WHAT???

For thirty days he couldn't pray?

Whatever would he do?

There was only one thing he COULD do, Daniel decided.

PRAY.

And he did. Three times a day—morning, noon and night, he checked his watch—eh—his hourglass—oops, his SUN-DIAL—to see if it was time to pray. And he knelt by his window and talked to God. And he listened to God, too.

"Now we've GOT him!" the governors cried. And they went to the king.

"Oh king!" they said. "Daniel has BROKEN YOUR LAW. Three times a day he PRAYS TO HIS GOD! And you signed that law. And it can't be changed!"

It was true.

Once the king signed a law, it could NOT be changed.

But it was a very very sad king who allowed Daniel to be arrested and taken to the lions' den.

"May your God save you, Daniel!" he cried.

And so it was done.

The guards lowered Daniel down

down

down—

Into the darkness. And they rolled a great stone over the mouth of the pit.

And there Daniel stood, alone, in the dark.

First he could hear the lions moving around him, swish-

ing their tails. And then he could see their eyes glowing like coals in the darkness.

And they came closer—

And closer—

And CLOSER.

And Daniel knew his faith was going to get its greatest test. Would God deliver him?

And then suddenly—

He saw something else.

A strange light.

It grew brighter. And brighter. And BRIGHTER.

And then he realized what it was.

An ANGEL!!! Standing between him—and the LIONS!

Back in the palace, all night long the king paced the floor of his chambers. He couldn't eat, he couldn't sleep. And in the lions' den, all night long—those lions paced back and forth, back and forth, back and forth—held back by the angel!

Early in the morning before it was hardly light, the king went to the lions' den. The guards pushed the stone away. And the king peered down into the darkness.

"Daniel!" he cried, "was your God able to deliver you from the lions? ARE YOU ALL RIGHT?!!?"

And then he heard a voice out of the darkness—

"I'm ALIVE, sire!"

It was Daniel!

"Are you hurt?" the king cried.

"No, sire! Not a scratch!" Daniel said. "God sent an ANGEL to watch over me!"

Oh JOY!

It was a very happy king who ordered the guards to pull Daniel back up out of the pit.

"Pull him UP!" he shouted.

And they did.

"There's not a scratch on him!" the king shouted again. "For his God is the LIVING God who rescued him from the lions! Let everyone tremble before the God of DANIEL!!!"

And so Daniel passed his biggest test of all.

He had obeyed God.

But then Daniel had been obeying God all his life, from the time—way back there when he was a BOY—a strapping lad—

Healthy—

Strong—

And very very smart.

But Daniel was something else too!

He was a man who talked to God.

And not only that.

He LISTENED to God.

And not only THAT.

He OBEYED God!

ALL RIGHT—

If you could go to a far away land and live in a palace and have anything you wanted—BUT—you would have to do everything all the other people did, and some of the things were no-no's—and IF you did them, you would be disobeying God—

What would YOU do?

Would you talk to God about it the way Daniel did?

Would you talk to God once a day?

Twice a day?

THREE times a day?

How many times a day WOULD you talk to God?

Think about it!

NOW FIND THIS STORY IN YOUR BIBLE

It's in Daniel, chapters 1 and 6.

A BIBLE VERSE TO LEARN

When we talk to God, we may tell Him thank you for the good things He gives us.

Give thanks to the Lord, for He is good; for His lovingkindness is everlasting (Ps. 136:1, *NASB*).

LET'S TALK TO GOD

Dear God, we're so glad that we can talk to you any time, day or night, and anywhere—at church, at home, at school, outside when we're playing—and you hear us. Thank you for listening to us. In Jesus' name, Amen.

Light Up the Skies!
JESUS IS BORN

What do you suppose was the first thing your mother and father did, after you were born?

Why they TOLD everybody about it!

They phoned all your grandparents and aunts and uncles and they sent announcement cards and telegrams to their friends who lived far away.

And they told everyone all about you—how much you weighed and whether you had hair yet and how many inches long you were—and OF COURSE they told everybody that you were the most BEAUTIFUL baby that had ever been born.

This is a story of the most important baby in all the world, and He was born way back when there were no phones or telegrams.

And do you know WHO told everybody about it?

GOD!

For the baby was His Son.

JESUS!

And do you know who were the first persons God told? And do you know HOW God told them?

Well, that's what this story is all about.

It happened two thousand years ago. In the middle of the night.

The place?

In the fields outside the city of Bethlehem.

And what and who were there?

Sheep! Hundreds of sheep. And lambs—middle-sized lambs and baby lambs and newborn lambs.

And of course, shepherds.

It was dark and quiet—so quiet you could hear a blade of grass if it shivered in the breeze. Every once in awhile, a baby lamb would wake up and go "Baaaa," and its mother would lick its face and say "Shhhhhh"—and it would go back to sleep again. But though it was dark, they weren't afraid. There was a fire crackling nearby and they knew that their shepherds were watching over them. They were all tucked in for a good night's sleep.

When suddenly—

Some of the older sheep woke up with a snort. And their noses wiggled. And their heads went up. And when the baby lambs saw their mothers and fathers and uncles and aunts with their heads up—

Their heads went up too.

Something strange was going on. What was it?

And then they saw it.

Woooooops! WHO was it?

He was like nobody they had ever seen before.

The shepherds saw it too.

And they got to their feet.

And then they sat back down again.

They were frightened.

They quivered and they shivered and they shook.

And the baby lambs!

THEY were so frightened they tried to crawl right underneath their mothers.

"Do you see what I see?" they asked each other.

"Yes, I see him. Do you see him too?"

"Yes, I see him too."

And the shepherds asked the same question. "Do you see what I see?"

"Yes!"

And they were AFRAID.

For what they saw was an ANGEL! An angel right there before their eyes! What did he want?

The angel wanted to make an ANNOUNCEMENT, is what he wanted.

THE GREATEST ANNOUNCEMENT IN THE WORLD.

LIGHT UP THE SKIES!

Yes—before their very eyes, there was a light in the sky, so bright that the fire that was crackling away seemed dim by comparison. The shepherds put their hands over their eyes and shivered and quivered some more. And the little lambs tried to crawl farther under their mothers, in fear and trembling. They were more afraid—all of them—than they had ever been in all their lives.

"Don't be afraid," the angel said. "I have good news! A BABY has been born tonight."

A baby? A BABY??!?!?

"Yes, a baby," the angel said. "The most important baby in all the world."

"Important baby?" the shepherds said, struggling to their feet.

"A very SPECIAL baby," the angel said. "A SAVIOUR. His name is Jesus."

A Saviour? Could this be true?

"It's true," the angel said, as if he could read their very thoughts. "He is in Bethlehem, right this very minute. He's in a stable—all wrapped up and tucked in—lying in a manger."

Then suddenly—

THE SKY WAS FULL OF ANGELS! AND THEY WERE PRAISING GOD!

"Do you hear what I hear?" the little lambs asked each other as they poked their noses out from underneath their mothers.

And, "Do you hear what I hear?" the shepherds asked each other too.

The angels were singing in a great swelling chorus— "GLORY TO GOD IN THE HIGHEST, AND ON EARTH PEACE, GOOD WILL TOWARD MEN!"

And the lambs and the sheep and the shepherds had never never in all their lives heard any sound as wonderful as this. The shepherds covered their eyes against the blinding light. And they fell on their knees to the ground. It was all so wonderful that they felt they could not STAND any more, when suddenly—

The angel who had been speaking to them—DISAPPEARED.

And the angels in the sky—DISAPPEARED.

And the light—DISAPPEARED.

And it was dark again.

There was no music.

There were no voices.

There was no sound, except the crackling of the shepherds' little fire.

The little lambs looked at their mothers and fathers and aunts and uncles. And the shepherds looked at each other.

It must be true. It MUST be true. An ANGEL had told them.

"There's only one way to be sure," the shepherds told each other. "We must go to Bethlehem and find out."

And they did!*

The shepherds who went, stumbled across the fields and huffed and puffed UP the hills and skidded DOWN the hills sending little stones racing ahead of them.

They got to Bethlehem huffing and puffing—

And went through the gates—

And sneaked through the streets—

And then—

They found it.

The stable.

They looked in the doorway.

There were sheep and goats and cows. And there was Jesus' mother, Mary. And there was Mary's husband Joseph. And there was a manger.

And there—and there—

Sure enough! There He was—all wrapped up and tucked in—

Baby Jesus!

*I'm sure they left a couple of shepherds behind to watch the sheep.

They HAD to believe it. For they had heard it from the angels—and now they could SEE him with their own eyes!

First they knelt down to worship Jesus, filled with love.

And then they went back through the streets filled with excitement.

And then they went back to their sheep filled with wonder.

For the most important baby in all the world had been born. And they'd got the announcement right out of the sky!

Oh yes.

One thing more.

The shepherds didn't keep this announcement all to themselves. They told everybody they met!

For good news like this was not just for the shepherds.

It was for EVERYBODY!

NOW FIND THIS STORY IN YOUR BIBLE

It's in Luke, chapter 2.

A BIBLE VERSE TO LEARN

For unto you is born this day in the city of David a Saviour, which is Christ the Lord (Luke 2:11, *KJV*).

LET'S TALK TO GOD

Dear God, we thank you that you loved us so much that you sent us the Lord Jesus to be our Saviour. We thank you that we can read the good news about Jesus in the Bible. In Jesus' name, Amen.

_____

Stop in Your Tracks!
JESUS AND THE TEN LEPERS

What has Jesus done for you this week?
Helped you get your homework done?
   Helped you have a lot of fun?
      Helped you learn when you felt dumb?
         Gave you things to make you glad?
            Cheered you up when you were sad?
            Made you well when you felt bad?
Wait a minute—WAIT A MINUTE.
Stop in your tracks.

It's easy enough to remember to ASK Jesus for things. It isn't always as easy to remember to THANK Him for them.

This is a story about some people who had a little trouble with their "thank-yous." They lived back during the days when Jesus was here on earth. There were ten of them. And they all had one thing in common.

They were lepers.

Now lepers were people who had leprosy—a horrible disease that made sores all over their bodies. Sometimes it made them crippled. Sometimes it made them blind. But ALWAYS it made them lonely. For leprosy was CATCHING.*

They carried bells with them always. And they had to ring their bells to warn other people to stay away from them.

They couldn't work.

They couldn't live with their families.

All they could do was stand by the roadside or outside the gates of the city—and BEG.

And then one day—

Something happened—

That turned their lives topsy turvy, upside down and sideways!

Good news!

It spread all over the village. It spread all over the countryside.

Jesus was coming to town! He was on His way this very minute!

Oh JOY, the ten lepers thought, and then—

Oh NO.

They'd NEVER get close enough. They were not allowed to get in crowds. They would never be able to get close to Jesus—

Wait a MINute.

*The way measles is catching.

They stopped in their tracks.

They couldn't mingle with the crowd—

BUT THEY COULD SHOUT.

And that's exactly what they did.

The crowd was gathering outside the city, and getting noisier and noisier. The people were stumbling over each other and jumping up on their tip-toes so they could see if Jesus was really coming. When suddenly—

"It's true!" The cry rang through the air. "It's Jesus coming with some of His disciples!" And one person told another person and soon EVERYBODY knew it.

The ten lepers backed away to get out of everybody else's way. They couldn't get near anybody else. But they could shout! And shout they did!

"Jesus!" they cried out, "have mercy on us!"

And louder. "Jesus, have mercy on us!"

And louder. "JESUS HAVE MERCY ON US! JESUS, HAVE MER—"

Wait a minute.

Could it be true?

Jesus was stopping. He was looking over the heads of the crowd—

And right at the ten lepers!

The ten lepers stood, their mouths gaping open, their eyes boggling.

Jesus was looking right at them!

And then Jesus said a most surprising thing.

He did NOT say, "Yes I will heal you."

And He did NOT say, "You will be healed tomorrow."

And He did NOT say, "You will be healed next week."

He said—"Go to the Temple and show the priests THAT YOU ARE HEALED."

What? What? WHAT?

They looked at their sores. They looked at each other. What did Jesus mean, that they were healed? Their sores were still there!

Now it was pretty hard for them to believe that they were healed when they could still see their sores. But that's exactly what Jesus was telling them to do. Did He mean what He said? They looked back at Him. Yes, He sure did. They looked at each other again. What were they supposed to do?

What were they supposed to DO?

They were supposed to obey Jesus is what they were supposed to do.

And do you know what?

They DID.

They hurried off toward the Temple, ringing their warning bells to keep the people away. They went faster, ringing their bells. Then they went FASTER, ringing their bells. And then—

WAIT A MINUTE!

They stopped in their tracks.

What was this?

They started looking at each other. All ten of them.

The most ASTONISHING thing had happened.

"Your sores are gone!" one of them said to another.

"So are yours!" the other shouted back, his eyes boggling.

"So are yours," said another.

"They are?"

"Well so are yours."

"Mine too?"

"Yours too!"

"It's true!"

Now they were all talking at once. The most unbelievable thing had happened, for indeed their sores were gone.

Their skin was smooth and healthy.

The ones who were limping didn't limp any more.

The ones who were all stooped over were standing up straight as a ramrod.

The ones who were using crutches threw them away.

And the ones who had patches over their eyes took them off! Why they were all so healthy and strong now, they could have RUN all the way to the Temple. They started walking faster and faster.

"It's true!"

"Jesus healed us!"

"It's true!"

"Jesus—"

WAIT A MINUTE.

One of them stopped in his tracks. He must go back, he thought, and tell Jesus that his sores were gone. And he must remember to thank Him.

What's this? Only ONE?

One out of TEN?

Yes, one out of ten.

one—
  two—
    three—
      four—
        five—
          six—
            seven—
              eight—
                nine—
                  TEN lepers.

But only one leper stopped in his tracks and remembered that he should go back and thank Jesus.

The other nine lepers kept right on going faster and faster toward the Temple. So happy were they, and so excited, they didn't even notice the one who had stopped. They never even looked back.

And the one leper who had decided to go back, stood there in the road, and watched them until they disappeared in the distance.

And then he turned, and started to walk back to where Jesus was. First he walked slowly. Then he went a little faster. And then he went FASTER, until pretty soon he was LEAPING, running with all his might, hurrying back to Jesus. And before he scarcely knew it, he began to shout. He was shouting even before he got close enough to see Jesus in the crowd.

"Jesus!" he shouted. "Glory to God! I am healed!"

The people looked at him, their eyes bugging out.

He WAS healed.

They were so surprised that they stepped back to let him through.

He was still leaping in the air when he got right up to Jesus. And then he fell flat on the ground with his face down in the dust.

"He's healed," the whispers went through the crowd. "This man is really healed." One told another and another told another until the whole crowd was shouting at once—

"This is the man who was a leper! He's healed!"

And then—"Wait a minute," they said to each other. "Be quiet! Hush!"

"What is he saying?"

"I can't hear!"

"Hush! Shhhhhh!"

And everybody hushed everybody else until the whole crowd was silent, listening to hear what the leper was saying. They didn't want to miss a word.

"Thank you, Jesus, oh thank You, THANK You, Jesus," the leper was saying.

"What's this?" the people whispered to each other. "What is it he said?"

"He's thanking Jesus for healing him."

"Oh."

And they passed the good word through the crowd, one whispering to another.

"Jesus, thank you," the leper kept saying, and "THANK you," over and over and over again.

Jesus looked down at the leper. Then He looked to the left and He looked to the right and He looked straight ahead.

"Didn't I heal TEN lepers?" He said at last.

There was murmuring and mumbling through the crowd. Yes, of course, Jesus had healed ten lepers. They had all seen it. They had all heard Him tell the ten lepers to go to the Temple.

Jesus looked around sadly. "Then where are the other nine?" he said.

"Ohhhhhhhh," the people in the crowd said. Where WERE the other nine, indeed? And they clucked and murmured and went Sts sts sts, the way your parents do when you've done something wrong.

For a minute or two, all you could hear were the murmurings and the Sts sts stses. Then Jesus looked down at the leper. And He said, "Stand up." And the leper stood up straight until he could look right at Jesus.

"Go on your way now," Jesus said. "You no longer have

to stand on the edge of crowds. Or stay away from other people. You can go back to your family. You believed me when I told you that you were healed. Even though you could still see your sores, you believed ME. Your faith has made you well."

The leper turned to go. He walked slowly through the crowd. The people who had stepped back, closed in behind him.

Then he began to walk faster. Then he walked faster and FASTER, until he was leaping and running down the road, so anxious was he to get about the business of LIVING again. There were SO many things he wanted to do that he could hardly wait to get started. The list was so long, he didn't know what to do first!

Of course he had already done the most important thing. He had STOPPED IN HIS TRACKS.

And he had remembered.

And he had gone back to thank JESUS.

What has Jesus done for you this week?
Helped you get your homework done?
Helped you have a lot of fun?
Gave you things to make you glad?
Cheered you up when you were sad?
Then wait a minute—hold it—HOLD IT—
STOP IN YOUR TRACKS!
And remember—the first thing to do—
IS TO THANK JESUS!

NOW FIND THIS STORY IN YOUR BIBLE
It's in Luke 17:11-19.

A BIBLE VERSE TO LEARN

Giving thanks always for all things unto God and the Father in the name of our Lord Jesus Christ (Eph. 5:20, *KJV*).

LET'S TALK TO GOD

Dear God, thank you for making the ten lepers well. And thank you for helping us when we don't feel good and when we need you. Help us to remember to thank you for all the things you give us and do for us. In Jesus' name, Amen.

A Man Nobody Liked—Except—!
JESUS AND THE TAX COLLECTOR

"Nobody likes me!"

Did you ever say this to yourself? What do you mean, nobody likes you? What makes you think so?

"Ohhh, 'cause I can't do very many things and some things I don't do right—"

Oh come on, now, that's not true at all.

"Well my brothers and sisters—I don't think they like me very much.

"Nobody likes me—
   Everybody hates me—
 I'm going to the backyard—
   And eat wooley worms."

Oh come ON. God loves you. And He's given you lots of talents—

90

"Uh um."

A few talents?

"Uh um."

One talent?

"Uh um—I don't think so."

Nonsense! To God, you are a VERY IMPORTANT PERSON.

"Okay if you say so."

You know, there was a man back in Bible times who thought nobody liked him. And he was probably right—for not very many people did. Because he was, of all things, a TAX COLLECTOR. And back in those times, the tax collectors charged the people WAY more than they were supposed to.

So naturally, nobody liked them.

Not even a little bit.

It was all right to be a tax collector, IF YOU WERE AN HONEST ONE.

But that was the problem.

Most of those tax collectors were NOT.

And the man in our story? He wasn't honest either.

His name was Zacchaeus.

Well, anyhow, Zacchaeus went on collecting taxes and charging the people too much, and the more he collected, the richer he got.

And then, one day—something happened that changed his whole life—

The news spread like wildfire, up one street and down another. People passed the word along.

Jesus was in town!

Women heard it and left their bread abaking in their

ovens and ran to where the crowds were gathering.

Farmers heard it and left their fields and gardens and came arunning.

Merchants heard it and left their shops.

Fishermen heard it and left their nets.

EVERYBODY heard it.

Barbers and bakers—

And candlestick makers—

And men who made boats—

And men who sold coats—

AND TAX COLLECTORS.

Yes, tax collectors. Zacchaeus heard it too.

He got up from his tax-collecting table so quickly he spilled his money (he stopped to pick it up again you may be sure)—and he hurried out to where the crowds were.

Oh oh.

That was when the trouble began.

For the crowds were so thick—and there were SO many people, Zacchaeus couldn't get through. And he HAD to get through to the very FRONT, or he wouldn't see Jesus.

Why?

You've already guessed it?

Right. Zacchaeus was very very VERY short!

He squiggled and he squaggled and he wiggled and he waggled, but NOBODY would budge or lose his place to let little Zacchaeus through. And he couldn't just ASK to be let through. For nobody LIKED a tax collector!

Just how Zacchaeus got the idea we do not know; he must have been desperate. For surely a rich tax collector simply does NOT shimmy up trees. But that's exactly what Zacchaeus did!

He ran along the edge of the crowd until he found a huge

sycamore tree that spread its lofty branches clear across the road. And he—HUP!—shimmied up it for all the world as if he were a monkey, and—HUP!—crawled across the branch that stretched over the road. His knees were scratched but he didn't care.

NOW he'd see Jesus.

And he felt so smart about it all, that he quite forgot that if he got caught, people would make fun of him. After all, he was a CHIEF tax collector, and everybody in town knew him. And it would look pretty silly to see a chief tax collector up in a sycamore tree.

But Zacchaeus didn't stop to think about that.

So there he was, carefully hidden in the branches.

And there he stayed.

And there he waited.

And waited.

Then suddenly—

"Here He comes!"

"Here comes Jesus!"

"Here comes the Master!"

"JESUS!"

And mothers lifted their small children up in the air to see.

And fathers hiked their medium-sized children up on their shoulders to see.

And the bigger children stood on their tiptoes and stretched their necks to see.

Sure enough!

There He was!

And coming closer and CLOSER to the sycamore tree!

Zacchaeus' eyes were boggling nearly out of his head. And then—oops.

94

Jesus was right UNDER the sycamore tree.

Jesus was STOPPING.

Jesus was looking UP!

Ooooooooooops. Jesus was looking right up at HIM.

EYEBALL TO EYEBALL!

And all the other people looked up too!

Oh good grief.

Zacchaeus' heart almost stopped beating.

He was undone!

But before Zacchaeus could say, "Undone" Jesus spoke.

"Zacchaeus!"

Zacchaeus almost fell right off his perch. Jesus had called him by name!

Astonishing!

And before Zacchaeus could say, "Astonishing" Jesus said, "Zacchaeus, come down—for I'm going to be a guest in your house today."

It was absolutely UNBELIEVABLE!

Jesus wanted to be his friend! And wanted to visit in his home!

Well Zacchaeus shimmied down that tree so fast—ouch!— that he had slivers to show for it, for weeks. And before you could say, "nobody-likes-a-tax-collector—"

Zacchaeus had whisked Jesus off to his home.

"I'm going to change," he said. "I'll never be the same again."

And he started giving orders to his servants.

"Kill a goat and roast it!" he shouted happily.

Then, to Jesus, "I'll give half my money to the poor."

Then, to the servants, "Bake some biscuits!"

And to Jesus, "If I've cheated anybody, I'll give him back FOUR TIMES more than I took from him!"

And to the servants, "Bring out the best cheese! And something to drink! And hurry!"

He bustled about happily, clapping his hands and giving orders.

"I'll be a changed man," he said. "I'll never be the same again. The MASTER is here in my house!"

And Zacchaeus was as good as his word.

He was indeed a changed man.

For he not only had Jesus in his HOUSE.

He invited Jesus into his LIFE.

And he was so kind and so honest after that—that it wasn't only Jesus who loved him.

Other people began to love him too!

You think nobody likes you?

Well, of course we ALL feel this way SOMETIMES. But it simply isn't true.

Why LOTS of people like you! They just haven't gotten around to telling you so!

And anyhow, Jesus loves you ALL THE TIME. To Him, you are a VERY IMPORTANT PERSON!

NOW FIND THIS STORY IN YOUR BIBLE

It's in Luke 19:1-10.

A BIBLE VERSE TO LEARN

Because God loves us, He promises to help us be the best persons we can be.

I can do everything through him who gives me strength (Phil. 4:13, *NIV*).

LET'S TALK TO GOD

Dear God, you have loved us for a long long time, even before we knew you. And you love us today. You tell us so in the Bible. Help us to welcome you into our home. We thank you for being with us and for living in our home and in our hearts. In Jesus' name, Amen.

What Was the First Easter Like?

JESUS IS RISEN

What's Easter like in your family? Do you wear new clothes? New shoes maybe? Anyhow, new clothes or not, do you get all scrubbed and dressed up and go to Sunday School and church?

Do you think the very first Easter was like that?

You do?

You DON'T?

Well what do you think the very first Easter WAS like? Do you think it was happy?

Well it turned OUT happy.

But the whole story didn't START OUT that way.

It started out—very sad.

For Jesus was dead.

His enemies had dragged Him through the streets of

Jerusalem, to a hill just outside the city. And they had nailed Him to a cross by His hands and feet. And they had put the cross in a great big hole dug in the ground, so it would stand up straight. And they had left Him to die.

Afterward, His friends had taken Him down from the cross and wrapped Him in clean clothes and carried Him tenderly to a garden tomb outside the city.*

Then soldiers had rolled an ENORMOUS stone over the entrance, and stayed there to guard the tomb. And all of Jesus' disciples had gone back to the city and gathered together in a room. And locked the door, so they could hide. They were frightened.

One day went by.

Two days went by.

And at the end of the second day—

One by one, the lights went out in all the houses in the city. And everything was dark. The garden where the tomb was, was dark too. The flowers had folded up their petals and gone to sleep for the night. Even the leaves on the trees were quiet. Nothing stirred. Not a leaf rustled. The birds had long ago tucked themselves in and were fast asleep.

The guards were outside the tomb, some of them standing, some of them sitting on the ground.

It was quiet, quiet, quiet.

Then SUDDENLY—

The earth began to tremble!

The soldiers got to their feet!

And then—in a twinkling of an eye—

An angel of the Lord came down from heaven! With the speed of sound he came, and seemed to split the sky! His

*The tomb was just like a cave. It was carved in the rocky hillside.

face shone like lightning! His clothing was a brilliant white! And before the horrified eyes of the soldiers, he went up to the great stone that closed the tomb.

And he touched it.

And his strength was so great, that with a little push, he ROLLED IT ASIDE!

It was open! THE TOMB WAS OPEN!

The soldiers fell back, shaking with fear.

And the angel looked at them—

Just LOOKED at them—

And they fell down like dead men!

Then it was all quiet again.

And then—slowly—the darkness began to go away. It got brighter. And the birds in their nests raised their heads and began stirring about. And the flowers began to unfold their petals.

It was early morning.

And then—

The sound of voices!

Women's voices!

There was Mary, the mother of James—

And Mary Magdalene—

And Joanna—

And Salome—

And some others too.

They had spices and perfumes with them for Jesus. And they hoped they'd find somebody to roll the stone away.

They came closer. And closer. Until they got to the garden.

And then—

They stopped.

The tomb was open! The tomb was OPEN! The great

stone was rolled aside! And Jesus was gone! And then—two angels appeared, right before their eyes!

The women just stood there as if they were nailed to the ground. They couldn't move.

"Don't be afraid," the angels said.

They couldn't move.

"He is alive. He is RISEN."

Still they couldn't move.

"He is RISEN," the angels went on, "just as He told you He would be."

This time they MOVED.

They ran and they RAN—back to the city.

First Mary Magdalene ran back. Then the others ran back.

And they told the disciples all about what had happened. And do you know WHAT?

The disciples didn't believe it! "Ha," they said, "you're telling fairy tales!"

But two of the disciples decided to go see for themselves. Their names were Peter and John.

They huffed and puffed all the way back to the garden tomb.

Then they stopped in their tracks.

The women were right.

The stone HAD been rolled away!

They went up to the entrance.

First they PEEKED in.

And then Peter STEPPED in. Right inside the tomb. And sure enough. Jesus was gone. The cloth He had been wrapped in was there, right before Peter's eyes, all neat and in order. And the cloth that had been wrapped around His head was there too, all folded up neatly.

They stared at each other in amazement. And they walked back to the city in wonder. Jesus was gone. But WHERE? And HOW? They couldn't imagine!

All day the disciples wondered. And they not only wondered—they were AFRAID.

And they weren't just a LITTLE BIT afraid.

They were so afraid that they got together in a big room and locked the door.

The morning went by.

The afternoon went by.

And evening came. And they ate their supper. And that's when it happened.

Suddenly—

Right there, before their very eyes—was JESUS!

Yes He WAS. Or WAS He? The doors were locked. How did He get in? Or—

WAS HE A GHOST?

They backed away, TERRIFIED.

And then—

"Why are you afraid?" He said. "I am really Jesus. Look at my hands." And He showed them His hands AND THEY HAD MARKS ON THEM FROM THE NAILS! Then He showed them His feet. MORE NAIL MARKS! IT WAS REALLY JESUS!

And as if THAT weren't enough to prove it, He stayed there and ate supper with them!

That was the first—

That was the first—

That was the FIRST Easter in all the world!

And it all happened because God loves us. And he wants us to be members of His family!

NOW FIND THIS STORY IN YOUR BIBLE

It's in Luke, chapters 23 and 24.

A BIBLE VERSE TO LEARN

Christ died for our sins according to the scriptures; and . . . he was buried, and . . . he rose again the third day according to the scriptures (1 Cor. 15:3,4, *KJV*).

LET'S TALK TO GOD

Dear God, we know that from the beginning of the world you planned to have your son Jesus die for us. And we know you planned to have Him rise from the dead. We thank you that you loved us so much that you let Jesus do this for us. In Jesus' name, Amen.

The Story Without an End
THE APOSTLES' SECRET WEAPON

Do you know when the church all began? Did you think it began when your mother first took you to Sunday School? And the teacher met you at the door?

"Good morning. I'm the third grade teacher. My name is Miss Flannelgraph."

"How do you do, Miss Flannelgraph," your mother says. "These are my children."

"Hello, Miss Flannelgraph."

"Hi, Miss Flannelgraph."

Did you think THAT's when church began?

Not so.

The church has been around for a long LONG time.

How long?

Ten years? Fifty years? A hundred?

No—TWO THOUSAND YEARS!

Was it a building with a cross on top?

No—it was PEOPLE.

It began with all the people who believed that Jesus was the Son of God. And that He rose from the dead. And that He was coming BACK again some day!

And who were those people? Why, they were Jesus' disciples, of course, and hundreds and hundreds of mothers and fathers and uncles and aunts and cousins and grandmothers and grandfathers and boys and girls. They were ALL in on it!

So the church wasn't a building and it didn't stay in one place. The church was PEOPLE and it went wherever THEY went.

And the story of the church is one of the oldest and most exciting stories in all the world!

BUT—

Do you know that from the minute the church BEGAN— there were people who tried to put an END to it? Imagine trying to END something before it hardly begins?

But that's exactly what happened.

For the church had—ENEMIES.

And who might these enemies be? Why the people who didn't believe in Jesus, that's who.

"We'll put an end to it!" their enemies cried, and, "WE'LL PUT AN END TO IT!" they bellowed. And they tried. They tried and they tried and they TRIED. But they could not do it. Because—

The church had a SECRET WEAPON!

And as long as they used that secret weapon, NOTHING could keep them from growing.

The things that happened to them would scare the fuzz right off a peach!

First, there were THREATS.

The first threat started over a MIRACLE, and it happened this way.

One day—

Two of the disciples were going to the Temple to pray. Their names were Peter and John, and they never suspected that they were going to bump right into a MIRACLE, but they did.

For at the gate of the Temple was a beggar. He sat there, cross-legged, his feet and ankles as limp as noodles. They had been that way from the day he was born—over forty years. There was no way that he could walk. He could only sit at the gate and beg passers-by for money.

And when Peter and John got up to him, that's what he did.

"Money!" he cried. "Please give me some money!"

And he held up his hands, "Money!"

Now most people who dropped money in his hands did it without even looking at him—just plopped a coin in his hands and hurried on. But Peter and John just STOPPED.

And looked at him, hard, eyeball to eyeball.

And then—and THEN—

"I have no money," Peter said, "but what I DO have—I'll give to you—RIGHT NOW." And before the beggar could figure out what was happening, Peter went on, "In the name of Jesus Christ—GET UP AND WALK!!!" And he took the beggar by his right hand and—

Woooooooosh!

—Pulled him to his feet!

The beggar stood there for a moment, swaying back and forth. And then he realized he could STAND. Then he took a wee step and he realized he could WALK. Then he took a bigger step and a bigger step and a BIGGER step—and he decided he could RUN—and even LEAP up in the air if he tried. And he tried—and he DID. His feet and ankles were as sturdy and strong as a track runner!

"Praise God!" he cried as he leaped again. "PRAISE GOD!" he yelled as he leaped his way into the Temple, and again, "PRAISE GOD!"

It was after that that the threats came. "No more speaking or teaching about Jesus!" the officials boomed when Peter and John were dragged before the court. "And no more miracles either—or ELSE!"

Well, the "or else" could mean anything from a whipping to prison—to death!

And THAT was enough to scare any ordinary Christian right into quitting on the spot!

But instead, Peter and John went back to their friends.

And they all used their secret weapon.

And the church kept growing.

The people ate together and worked together and shared their food and shared their clothing and NOTHING could make them discouraged.

But the threats weren't all.

THERE WAS ALSO DANGER.

Sometimes even the WEATHER seemed to be against them.

One time, one of them was sailing across the sea to take the message of Jesus to faraway lands. His name was Paul.

And this time, the problem wasn't other people.

This time it was a STORM.

One minute, the ship Paul was in was sailing along as nicely as you please, and the next minute—

The wind came swooping down from the north and

POUNCED like an angry GIANT, tearing at the sails and making the ship bob about like a cork on the end of a fishing line!

"Furl the sail—furl the sail!" The captain's orders rang out. And the sailors climbed the rigging and loosened the ropes and let the big sail down. But the huge waves tossed the ship up in the air and then hurled her down

down

down

into the trough.

again!

up

her

And then the next big wave hurled

"Cargo overboard! Cargo overboard!" the captain bellowed. And the sailors threw boxes and bales and bags of wheat and other cargo into the wild raging sea.

"Don't be afraid!" Paul shouted. "God has told me that not one of you will be killed! You'll all be saved—every one of you!"

And Paul KNEW.

For he had used the SECRET WEAPON!

But the storm grew worse. It drove the ship forward, sideways, and nearly upside down—until it finally—ran—into—A SANDBAR.

AND BEGAN TO COME APART!

There was CREAKING and SCRAPING and RIPPING and TWISTING AND CRUNCHING—

Then everybody on the ship slid and clawed and jumped and fell—until one way or another—they were all pitched into the raging sea!

Down
    they   again.
        went   came
            under   they
               the   up
                  water. And
And
    down   they came—until—finally—
       they   up
          went and

—Somehow they were all hurled up onto the beach!

And the storm—slowly—died—down.

And when they counted noses—not ONE of them was lost. They were all there, safe and sound!

So there were miracles and threats and prison and danger.

But the church kept growing as long as the people used their secret weapon.

What is the secret weapon? Haven't you guessed it yet?

Well, if you HAVEN'T guessed it already (and you probably have) you'll find out now.

This happened when Peter got thrown in prison for the um-tee-umpth time. But this time they weren't going to let him out. This time they were planning to KILL him.

The word spread all over Jerusalem.

All the Christians heard about it. Not just the grown-ups but the children and young people too.

There was one little servant girl who heard about it. Her name was Rhoda. One day Rhoda's mistress called—

"Rhoda, drop your baking for now and come help me. Some friends are coming here tonight to do something VERY IMPORTANT. We're all going to gather together and PRAY. For Peter."

"Yes ma'am," Rhoda said. And then the tears began to slide down her nose. "But ma'am, they're going to KILL Peter at the end of the week!"

"Rhoda, don't cry," her mistress said. "We're going to ask God to save Peter's life. Now Rhoda, dry your eyes and blow your nose and come help me. We must believe God."

"Yes ma'am," Rhoda said, fishing for her handkerchief. "I know I'm very young. But when the people come to pray could I sit on the side and listen? I don't know how to pray aloud very well, but I could pray for Peter in my heart."

"Of course you can, Rhoda," her mistress said. "Your prayers are VERY IMPORTANT. Now come. Let's get busy and get the house ready. They'll be here before too long."

Well, the people came that night, and the next night, and the NEXT night and the NEXT night—

And then came the saddest night of all. For the very next morning Peter was going to be killed!

Oh how hard Rhoda prayed!

But while she prayed, the tears were dripping off her nose for she knew that it was dark in Peter's cell. And that Peter was locked up and DOUBLE CHAINED to two soldiers, while more soldiers stood guard at the prison gate.

But what Rhoda DIDN'T know was—

Back in the prison, at that very moment, suddenly—

Peter's cell was ablaze with light! And there, standing over him, was an ANGEL!

"Quick! Get up!" the angel said, whacking Peter on the side to awaken him. Peter rubbed his eyes. Was he dreaming?

"Hurry!" cried the angel.

Peter decided this was no time to argue, so he scrambled

to his feet—and as he got up—HIS DOUBLE CHAINS fell off!

"Put on your belt," the angel said. "And your sandals. And your coat. And HURRY."

Peter scrambled into his clothes and followed the angel out to the hall. They walked along—right—past—the—soldiers!

And when they got to the iron gate that led to the street—it opened all by itself the way the supermarket doors open when you step up to them!

And the next thing Peter knew, he was out on the street—

And the angel was gone!

And THAT'S how it happened that back in the house where Rhoda lived—while the people were praying (and Rhoda was praying in her heart)—there was a knock on the courtyard gate!

What was THIS?

Rhoda was the first one on her feet. She flew out into the night and ran toward the gate. "Who is it?" she called out.

"Let me in!" a voice called back. "It's Peter!"

PETER???!!?!?!!?

Rhoda flew back into the house. "It's Peter!" she shouted. And no one would believe her!

"It IS Peter," she insisted. "I know his voice!"

Then they all began to talk at once.

"No!"

"They must have killed him already!"

"It must be his ghost!"

"Or maybe it's his guardian angel!"

"Noooooo," Rhoda cried, "IT'S PETER!"

They all got stuck in the doorway getting out there to open the gate.

And sure enough it WAS!

And were they ever HAPPY!

For they had used their secret weapon.

And, as you've already guessed, their secret weapon was PRAYER.

So in spite of threats and prison and danger—yes, and even death (for some of the Christians WERE killed)—

The church kept growing.

"We'll put an end to it!" their enemies bellowed as the grown-ups and the young people and the children shared their food and clothing and money and worked together and PRAYED together—

But there WAS no end to it—

And there IS no end to it—

And there WILL BE NO END TO IT—

Until Jesus comes again!!!

NOW FIND THIS STORY IN YOUR BIBLE

It's in Acts, chapters 3 and 4.

A BIBLE VERSE TO LEARN

This Bible verse describes how people in the church should act toward each other.

Let all be harmonious, sympathetic, brotherly, kind-hearted, and humble in spirit (1 Pet. 3:8 *NASB*).

LET'S TALK TO GOD

Dear God, teach us to use the secret weapon you have given to us. Thank you that we can pray when we are happy, when we are scared, when we are sick, when we sin and all the other times. And thank you for the church where we can learn about you and Jesus. In Jesus' name, Amen.

It's Hard to Be Nice to People Who Aren't
PAUL AND SILAS IN PRISON

Do you know what missionaries are?

What?

Little pins stuck in a map on the wall of your Sunday School?

Oh come on, now. Missionaries aren't pins—they're PEO-PLE. You knew that all the time, didn't you?

Missionaries are people who travel, go off to faraway places to tell people about Jesus. Now it would be easy to go off and tell people about Jesus if the people were always NICE, if everybody was kind to you and you didn't have any trouble. But what if everybody WASN'T nice? What if they gave you a lot of trouble? And what if they were CRUEL to you? Would you still be able to love them?

Well, there were two missionaries who went on a journey

to tell people about Jesus and the people were cruel to THEM. Let's find out what the missionaries did about it.

Their names were Paul and Silas and they lived a long time ago, back in Bible days. And they packed their duffle bags and went off to be missionaries. And they traveled and traveled from city to city and told people about Jesus.

Now ONE day—

They went to the city of Philippi. Just think of the name "Philip" and add "I."

ANYHOW.

They were walking through the streets of Philippi, minding their business when—WHOOPS!

Suddenly they were grabbed from behind and dragged along the streets. First a few people gathered around. Then more people gathered. And then a LOT of people gathered, and soon there was a GREAT CROWD.

"Arrest these men!" they shouted. "Arrest them! ARREST THEM! Take them to the market place! Take them to the judges!"

And sure enough, Paul and Silas were half pushed and half dragged clear into the market place. And there, upon a platform, on great big chairs, were the judges. Alongside them were big soldiers with big muscles and big wooden WHIPS.

And the crowd shouted again. "ARREST them!" they bellowed.

"Order! Order!" the judges cried back. And the mob grew silent. "What is the charge?" the judges asked. "What have these men done?"

"These men are upsetting everything in the city! They are teaching people about Jesus! They are doing things that are against our Roman law!" the people shouted back.

Oh oh. That did it.

The judges said, "Hmmmmmmmmf," and "Mmmmm-mmmmph."

And then they said, "Beat them with rods! And throw them in prison!"

And the big soldiers with the wooden whips stood by while some attendants dragged Paul and Silas over to the whipping posts and tied their hands to stakes.

Whoop! Down came the rods on their backs.

Wap! Down they came again, harder this time.

Wop! Down again, harder still.

WHOOOP! WAP! WHAM!

At last it was over. The attendants untied Paul and Silas and soldiers dragged them off to prison.

The prison was an ugly stone building with thick walls and huge heavy doors. As the soldiers brought Paul and Silas up to it, the jailer came running out from his house next door.

"Who do we have here?" the jailer called out.

"Prisoners!" the soldiers called back. "For you!"

"What have they done?"

"HO HO! What have they DONE? Why these are the men who can tell you how to have your sins forgiven! They show the way to be saved!"

"The way to be saved, eh?" said the jailer. "That's a new one."

"Yeah, it's a new one, all right," the soldiers said. "Lock them up. See that they don't get out. If they do escape, you're apt to lose your head!"

"I know, I know," the jailer said. "I'll keep them safe all right. I'll put them in the INNER DUNGEON."

And he unlocked the big door of the jail by lifting the

heavy bars out of their slots, and the soldiers dragged Paul and Silas inside.

Ohhhhhh, it was DARK inside. And it smelled BAD.

Then the jailer went to the door of the INNER DUNGEON. He unlocked it. And he opened it. And the soldiers dragged Paul and Silas in, and put their feet in big wooden frames that also locked by putting big bars in slots. And they closed the door. And locked it. And Paul and Silas were left alone in the dark.

And the minutes went by.

And the hours went by.

And finally it was almost midnight.

Paul spoke to his friend in the darkness. "Silas," he said, "are you asleep?"

"No, no—I'm awake," Silas answered.

"Well God isn't asleep either," Paul said. "I've been sitting here thinking. God isn't asleep. He's still watching over us."

"Why that's RIGHT," Silas whispered back. "The God who watches over us will NEVER sleep, day or night. He never even takes a NAP."

"That's what I was thinking," said Paul.

And he began to SING.

Yes he did!

And Silas joined in.

"Praise the Lord," they shouted. And they sang songs and hymns and then they set Bible verses to music. Probably neither of them could carry a tune in a bushel basket, but they sang anyway! They sang as if they expected God to get them out of that prison any minute. As if God—

Wait a minute! What was that? Thunder? It was a rumble. Wait a minute!

The ground was shaking!

The walls of the prison were swaying back and forth!

The wooden bars in the door began to jiggle and joggle up and down until—until—THEY JOGGLED RIGHT OUT OF THEIR SLOTS! It was an earthquake! EARTHQUAAAAAAAAAAKE!!!

Now the floor of the prison was going up and down crazily, like the waves in the ocean. And the wooden bars that were binding Paul and Silas' feet jiggled and joggled up and down until—until—THEY joggled right out of THEIR slots!

Their feet were free!

Paul and Silas helped each other up. Then with a great g-r-o-a-n, the dungeon door flew open! Then the outer doors! They just FLEW open!

Then they heard the jailer shouting outside. He had stumbled from his house along the rocking ground. And he had gotten to the door of the prison and had seen that it was open!

The ground was not shaking now. The earthquake was over.

But there was not a prisoner in sight.

"They escaped!" the jailer thought. "They escaped!" And he drew his sword to kill himself.

And then—

"HOLD IT!" Paul called out. "Don't harm yourself! We have not escaped—we're all here!"

The jailer whirled around.

He stood there in the dark for a moment.

Then, "Lights!" he bellowed. "BRING ME SOME LIGHTS!"

The guards came arunning with flaming torches. The

jailer grabbed one and hurried into the prison. And there stood the prisoners. And there stood Paul and Silas. They had not tried to escape.

Then the jailer remembered what the soldiers had told him. "These two prisoners are men who tell you how to have your sins forgiven—they tell you how to be SAVED!"

And the jailer fell down on his knees. "Oh sirs," he cried, "what must I do to be saved?"

Now Paul could have said, "Oh I don't think I'll tell you. After all you pushed me around and locked me in prison."

He COULD have said that.

But he didn't.

Instead, he said, "Believe on the Lord Jesus Christ and you will be saved. And that goes for your whole family too."

"I will!" the jailer cried, "I will! I do, right now."

And you know, right then and there they had a little prayer meeting!

Then the jailer turned to the guards. "Guards," he said. "Help these poor men up to my house. I want my family to hear about this."

And that's exactly what happened. The jailer's family washed the places on Paul and Silas' back where they had been whipped. And they gave them food to eat.

And Paul and Silas told them all about Jesus.

And the next day Paul and Silas were allowed to go on their way.

Now Paul and Silas COULD have said, "Let's quit this missionary business. We're tired of being beaten. And prison! Who needs it?"

But they didn't. Instead, they kept right on traveling and telling people about Jesus.

For their hearts were filled with Jesus' love.

NOW FIND THIS STORY IN YOUR BIBLE

It's in Acts, chapter 16.

A BIBLE VERSE TO REMEMBER

And [Jesus] said unto them, Go ye into all the world, and preach the gospel to every creature (Mark 16:15, *KJV*).

LET'S TALK TO GOD

Dear God, help us to remember that you never sleep. You are always awake, taking care of us. And thank you that we can be saved when we believe on the Lord Jesus Christ. Help us to tell all our friends how they can be saved too. In Jesus' name, Amen.

"It's Good to Give Thanks"

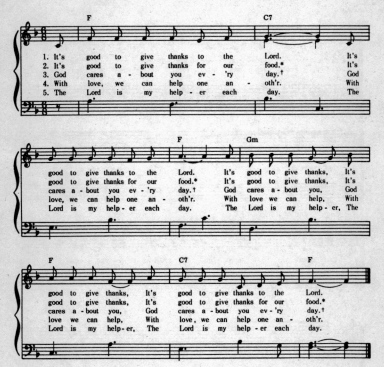

1. It's good to give thanks to the Lord. It's
2. It's good to give thanks for our food.* It's
3. God cares a-bout you ev-'ry day.† God
4. With love, we can help one an-oth'r. With
5. The Lord is my help-er each day. The

good to give thanks to the Lord. It's good to give thanks, It's
good to give thanks for our food.* It's good to give thanks, It's
cares a-bout you ev-'ry day.† God cares a-bout you, God
love, we can help one an-oth'r. With love we can help, With
Lord is my help-er each day. The Lord is my help-er, The

good to give thanks, It's good to give thanks to the Lord.
good to give thanks, It's good to give thanks for our food.*
cares a-bout you, God cares a-bout you ev-'ry day.†
love we can help, With love, we can help one an-oth'r.
Lord is my help-er, The Lord is my help-er each day.

Words: Scripture. Music: Traditional.

Stanzas references: 1. Psalm 92:1
3. 1 Peter 5:7
4. Galatians 5:13
5. Hebrews 13:6

* Substitute names of other things for which children may thank God, such as legs, arms, family members, etc.

† Substitute name of a child for the words "ev'ry day."

Arrangement © 1971 by G/L Publications.

"I'm a Special Person"

1. I'm a spe-cial per-son, There's no one like me.
2. God made each one diff'-rent, No one is the same.

I'm glad I am (___Your Name___) That's my name! That's me!
God knows all a-bout me. He e-ven knows my name.

God thinks I am spe-cial, He thinks you're spe-cial, too.

He loves us 'cause I am me and you are you.

Words: Margaret M. Self. Music: Traditional.